PRESIDENTIAL
WIT & WISDOM

MEMORABLE QUOTES FROM
GEORGE WASHINGTON TO BARACK OBAMA

EDITED BY JOSLYN PINE

DOVER PUBLICATIONS, INC.
MINEOLA, NEW YORK

*To my parents,
in loving memory*

Bibliographical Note

Presidential Wit & Wisdom: Memorable Quotes from George Washington to Barack Obama, first published in 2009, is a revised and updated version of *Wit and Wisdom of the American Presidents: A Book of Quotations*, first published by Dover Publications, Inc., in 2001.

International Standard Book Number
ISBN-13: 978-0-486-47153-2
ISBN-10: 0-486-47153-5

Manufactured in the United States by Courier Corporation
47153502
www.doverpublications.com

Note

"If men were angels," remarked James Madison in the 51st Federalist Paper, "no government would be necessary." This notion at least partially expressed the sentiments of the Founding Fathers as they sought to shape the government of the young nation at the Constitutional Convention in Philadelphia in 1787. Yet it is just as true to say that they were equally mistrustful of too much authority. Their ultimate solution, therefore, was to achieve a balance by defining a strong central authority that was limited in its ability to abuse power.

While constitutional provisions for the legislative branch are described in meticulous detail, the American Constitution is rather vague and ambiguous on the subject of presidential powers. Some, of course, are enumerated, such as the role of commander in chief of the armed forces, the authority to grant pardons and reprieves, the veto power over legislation, as well as the ability to make treaties with the consent of the Senate, and to appoint judges and ambassadors.

In fact, as our history has unfolded, this lack of precise definition for the executive branch has been fortuitous. It has allowed the presidency to evolve through both historical circumstance and in accordance with the special gifts of the individual at the helm. Those presidents held in highest esteem by historians, such as George Washington, Abraham Lincoln, Woodrow Wilson, and Franklin D. Roosevelt, filled the office when far-reaching powers were demanded in order for the nation to survive times of crisis. Many others, while not so critically challenged by the turmoil of events, still managed to distinguish themselves as the movers and shakers of their times.

Here, history is indeed biography as we reflect on the story of America as also the story of her presidents. Their own words mark the great themes in American history as well as mark them as remarkable men.

Are these quotes, in fact, in "their own words"? In earlier decades of the nation's history, speeches were generally more widely read in newspapers than delivered aloud to live audiences. Inevitably, this shaped their form and content. There existed then informal relationships among presidents and their colleagues, who were sometimes called upon to contribute literary advice—and sometimes their ghostwriting skills—for the composition of speeches. It wasn't until 1920, when radio broadcasting was in its infancy, that the mass-media revolution began to unfurl and eventually transformed presidential speechwriting into a profession in its own right.[*] Nevertheless, we may take on faith that all the quotes that follow reflect in some quintessential way on the individual who penned and/or uttered them.

Since many different sources were consulted in compiling these quotations, punctuation has, for the most part, been modernized and standardized for the sake of clarity and consistency. Chronological order was not an organizing principle here because many of the source quotes were undated. And since four different sources might each contain a different version of the same quote, every effort has been made to present the version closest to the spirit and substance of the original.

[*]Robert Schlesinger, *White House Ghosts: Presidents and Their Speechwriters* (New York: Simon & Schuster, Inc., 2008), 1–4.

PRESIDENTIAL
WIT & WISDOM

MEMORABLE QUOTES FROM
GEORGE WASHINGTON TO BARACK OBAMA

★ ★ ★ ★ ★ ★ ★

George Washington

Born February 22, 1732 — Died December 14, 1799

1st President, 1789–1797 ★ Federalist

*Labor to keep alive in your breast
that little spark of celestial fire,
called conscience.*

☆☆☆☆☆

Of all the animosities which have existed among mankind, those which are caused by a difference of sentiments in religion appear to be the most inveterate and distressing, and ought most to be deprecated.

Few men have virtue
enough to withstand the
highest bidder.

Discipline is the soul of
an army. It makes small numbers
formidable; procures success to
the weak, and esteem to all.

I hope I shall possess firmness and virtue enough to maintain what I consider the most enviable of all titles, the character of an honest man.

A slender acquaintance with the world must convince every man that actions, not words, are the true criterion of the attachment of friends; and that the most liberal professions of goodwill are very far from being the surest marks of it.

[*attributed*]

Father, I cannot tell a lie.
I did it with my little hatchet.

6   *George Washington*

*B*e courteous to all but intimate with few, and let those few be well tried before you give them your confidence; true friendship is a plant of slow growth, and must undergo and withstand the shocks of adversity before it is entitled to the appellation.

★ ★ ★

*A*t a distance from the theatre of action, truth is not always related without embellishment.

George Washington 7

Associate yourself with
men of good quality if you
esteem your own reputation, for
'tis better to be alone than
in bad company.

★ ★ ★

As the first of everything in our
situation will serve to establish a
precedent, it is devoutly wished on
my part, that these precedents may
be fixed on true principles.

[on taking the oath of office]

I walk on untrodden ground.
There is scarcely any part of my
conduct that may not hereafter be
drawn into precedent.

———★———

Patriotism . . . must be aided by a
prospective interest or some reward.
For a time, it may of itself push men
into action, to bear much, to encounter
difficulties. But it will not endure
unassisted by interest.

George Washington   9

☆☆☆☆

My ardent desire is, and my aim has been, to comply strictly with all our engagements, foreign and domestic; but to keep the United States free from political connections with every other country, to see them independent of all and under the influence of none.

☆☆☆☆

★ ★ ★ ★ ★ ★ ★

John Adams

Born October 30, 1735 — Died July 4, 1826
2nd President, 1797–1801 ★ Federalist

*I would define liberty to be a power
to do as we would be done by.*

☆☆☆☆

Posterity! You will never know how much it cost the present generation to preserve your freedom! I hope you will make good use of it! If you do not, I shall repent it in Heaven that I ever took half the pains to preserve it!

☆☆☆☆

12 *John Adams*

Power naturally grows. Why?
Because human
passions are insatiable.

The jaws of power are always
open to devour, and her arm is
always stretched out, if possible,
to destroy the freedom of thinking,
speaking, and writing.

John Adams 13

*E*very project has been found no better than committing the lamb to the custody of the wolf, except that one which is called balance of power.

The preservation of the
means of knowledge
among the lowest ranks
is of more importance
than all the property
of all the rich men in
the country.

It is weakness rather than
wickedness which renders
men unfit to be trusted
with unlimited power.

I must study politics and
war that my sons may have
liberty to study mathematics
and philosophy.

You will never be alone with a
poet in your pocket.

———★———

Liberty, according to my
metaphysics, is a self-determining
power in an intellectual agent.
It implies thought, choice,
and power.

☆☆☆☆

Ambition is the subtlest beast
of the intellectual and moral
field. It is wonderfully adroit in
concealing itself from its owner.

☆☆☆☆

★ ★ ★ ★ ★ ★ ★

Thomas Jefferson

Born April 13, 1743 — Died July 4, 1826

3rd President, 1801–1809 ★ Democratic-Republican

I'm a great believer in luck,
and I find the harder I work
the more I have of it.

☆☆☆☆☆

If congressmen talk too much, how can it be otherwise in a body to which the people send one hundred and fifty lawyers, whose trade it is to question everything, yield nothing, and talk by the hour.

Whenever a man has cast a
longing eye on offices,
a rottenness begins in his conduct.

In matters of principle, stand
like a rock; in matters of taste,
swim with the current.

Thomas Jefferson   21

Question with boldness even the existence of God; because, if there be one, he must more approve of the homage of reason than that of blindfolded fear.

Laws are made for men of ordinary understanding, and should therefore be construed by the ordinary rules of common sense. Their meaning is not to be sought for in metaphysical subtleties, which may make anything mean everything or nothing, at pleasure.

Ignorance of the law is not an excuse
in any country. If it were,
the laws would lose their effect,
because it can always be pretended.

☆☆☆☆

The tree of liberty must be refreshed
from time to time with the
blood of patriots and tyrants.
It is its natural manure.

We are not to expect to be translated from despotism to liberty in a feather bed.

The second office of the government is honorable and easy; the first is but a splendid misery.

It does me no injury for my neighbor to say there are twenty gods or no God. It neither picks my pocket nor breaks my leg.

Thomas Jefferson

The time to guard against corruption and tyranny is before they shall have gotten hold of us. It is better to keep the wolf out of the fold than to trust to drawing his teeth and talons after he shall have entered.

★ ★ ★

I sincerely believe that banking establishments are more dangerous than standing armies, and that the principle of spending money to be paid by posterity, under the name of funding, is but swindling futurity on a large scale.

Thomas Jefferson 27

It behooves every man
who values liberty of
conscience for himself,
to resist invasions of it in
the case of others.

★ ★ ★

Timid men prefer the
calm of despotism to the
boisterous sea of liberty.

If I could not go to heaven but with a party, I would not go there at all.

It is in our lives and not from our words, that our religion must be read.

☆☆☆☆☆

We hold these truths to be self-evident,—that all men are created equal; that they are endowed by their creator with certain inalienable rights; that among these are life, liberty, and the pursuit of happiness.

★ ★ ★ ★ ★ ★ ★

James Madison

Born March 16, 1751 — Died June 28, 1836

4th President, 1809–1817 ★ Democratic-Republican

*The diffusion of knowledge
is the only guardian of true liberty.*

☆☆☆☆☆

Since the general civilization of mankind, I believe there are more instances of the abridgement of the freedom of the people, by gradual and silent encroachments of those in power, than by violent and sudden usurpations.

[*on the Constitution*]

Every word decides a question
between power and liberty.

It is a melancholy reflection that
liberty should be equally exposed
to danger whether the government
have too much or too little power.

James Madison   33

*P*erhaps it is a universal truth that the loss of liberty at home is to be charged to provisions against danger, real or pretended, from abroad.

Temporary deviations from fundamental principles are always more or less dangerous. When the first pretext fails, those who become interested in prolonging the evil will rarely be at a loss for other pretexts.

Religious bondage shackles and debilitates the mind, and unfits it for every noble enterprise.

*J*ustice is the end of government. It is the end of civil society. It ever has been and ever will be pursued until it be obtained, or until liberty be lost in the pursuit.

★ ★ ★

*B*ut what is government itself, but the greatest of all reflections on human nature? If men were angels, no government would be necessary.

James Madison 37

Conscience is the most sacred of all property.

★ ★ ★

Having outlived so many of my contemporaries, I ought not to forget that I may be thought to have outlived myself.

★ ★ ★ ★ ★ ★ ★

James Monroe

Born April 28, 1758 — Died July 4, 1831

5th President, 1817–1825 ★ Democratic-Republican

*Preparation for war is a constant stimulus
to suspicion and ill-will.*

★ ★ ★ ★

The history of all ages proves that . . .
at least one half of every century,
in ancient as well as modern times,
has been consumed in wars, and
often of the most general and
desolating character.

★ ★ ★ ★

40   *James Monroe*

The circulation of confidence
is better than the circulation
of money.

In a government founded on the
sovereignty of the people,
the education of youth is an
object of the first importance.

James Monroe 41

*I*n this great nation
there is but one order,
that of the people.

The revolution of France undoubtedly took its origin from that of the United States. Her citizens fought and bled within our service. They caught the spirit of liberty here, and carried it home with them.

[Monroe Doctrine]

The American continents . . .
are henceforth not to be considered
as subjects for future colonization
by any European powers.

Let us, by all wise and
constitutional measures, promote
intelligence among the people,
as the best means of preserving
our liberties.

★ ★ ★ ★ ★ ★ ★

John Quincy Adams

Born July 11, 1767 — Died February 23, 1848
6th President, 1825–1829 ★ Democratic-Republican

To believe all men honest would be folly.
To believe none so is something worse.

☆☆☆☆

[on the presidency]

I can scarcely conceive a more harassing, wearying, teasing condition of existence. It literally renders life burdensome. What retirement will be I cannot realize, but have formed no favorable anticipation. It cannot be worse than this perpetual motion and crazing cares.

I had much rather you should impute to me great error of judgment than the smallest deviation from sincerity.

Always vote for a principle, though you vote alone, and you may cherish the sweet reflection that your vote is never lost.

Our Constitution professedly
rests upon the good sense and
attachment of the people.
This basis, weak as it may appear,
has not yet been found to fail.

48   *John Quincy Adams*

$\mathcal{T}$he soul of one man cannot by human law be made the property of another. The owner of a slave is the owner of a living corpse; but he is not the owner of the man.

★ ★ ★

$\mathcal{I}$ consider an unjust war as the greatest of all human atrocities, but I esteem a just one as the highest of all human virtues.

There is nothing so deep and nothing so shallow which political enmity will not turn to account.

★ ★ ★

Law logic—an artificial system of reasoning, exclusively used in the courts of justice, but good for nothing anywhere else.

50   *John Quincy Adams*

★ ★ ★ ★ ★ ★ ★

Andrew Jackson

Born March 15, 1767 — Died June 8, 1845

7th President, 1829–1837 ★ Democrat

*One man with courage
makes a majority.*

☆☆☆☆

The murderer only takes the life of the parent and leaves his character as a goodly heritage to his children, whilst the slanderer takes away his goodly reputation and leaves him a living monument to his children's disgrace.

☆☆☆☆

Mere precedent is a dangerous source of authority.

We have all read history, and is it not certain, that of all aristocracies mere wealth is the most odious, rapacious, and tyrannical?

*I*n a free government the demand for moral qualities should be made superior to that of talents.

There are, perhaps,
few men who can for any
length of time enjoy
office and power without
being more or less under
the influence of feelings
unfavorable to the faithful
discharge of their
political duties.

The wisdom of man never yet contrived a system of taxation that would operate with perfect equality.

$\mathscr{T}$he brave man inattentive to his duty,
is worth little more to his country than the
coward who deserts her in the hour of danger.

★ ★ ★

$\mathscr{T}$he moment a person forms a theory, his
imagination sees in every object only the traits
that favor that theory.

If such corruption exists
in the green tree, what will
be in the dry?

Heaven will be no heaven
to me if I do not meet
my wife there.

★ ★ ★ ★ ★ ★

Martin Van Buren

Born December 5, 1782 — Died July 24, 1862
8th President, 1837–1841 ★ Democrat

*As to the presidency, the two happiest days
of my life were those of my entry upon the
office and of my surrender of it.*

☆☆☆☆

Indebtedness cannot be lessened by borrowing more money, or by changing the form of the debt.

☆☆☆☆

Is it possible to be anything in this country without being a politician?

Most men are not scolded out of their opinion.

[*on slavery*]

No evil can result from its inhibition more pernicious than its toleration.

★ ★ ★ ★ ★ ★ ★

William Henry Harrison

Born February 9, 1773 — Died April 4, 1841

9th President, 1841 (served one month) ★ Whig

*Conscience is that magistrate of God in
the human heart whose still small voice the
loudest revelry cannot drown.*

★★★★★

If political parties in a republic are necessary to secure a degree of vigilance to keep the public functionaries within bounds of law and duty, at that point their usefulness ends.

The plea of necessity,
that eternal argument of all
conspirators.

Power is insinuating. Few men are
satisfied with less power than
they are able to procure. No lover
is ever satisfied with the first
smile of his mistress.

William Henry Harrison   65

★ ★ ★

[about himself]

Some folks are silly
enough to have formed a
plan to make a President
of the United States out of
this clerk and clodhopper.

★ ★ ★ ★ ★ ★ ★

John Tyler

Born March 29, 1790 — Died January 18, 1862
10th President, 1841–1845 ★ Whig

*The barking of newspapers
and the brawling of demagogues
can never drive me from my course.*

$\mathcal{P}$opularity, I have always thought, may aptly be compared to a coquette—the more you woo her, the more apt is she to elude your embrace.

Patronage is the sword and cannon by which war may be made on the liberty of the human race. . . . Give the President control over the purse—the power to place the immense revenues of the country into any hands he may please, and I care not what you call him, he is "every inch a king."

[campaign slogan]

Tippecanoe and Tyler, Too.

[inscription on the grave of his horse]

Here lies the body of my good horse, "The General." For twenty years he bore me around the circuit of my practice, and in all that time he never made a blunder. Would that his master could say the same!

★ ★ ★ ★ ★ ★ ★

James Knox Polk

Born November 2, 1795 — Died June 15, 1849

11th President, 1845–1849 ★ Democrat

Ours is not a consolidated empire,
but a confederated union.

★★★★★

The people of the United States have no idea of the extent to which the President's time, which ought to be devoted to more important matters, is occupied by the voracious and often unprincipled persons who seek office.

★★★★★

We have a country as well
as a party to obey.

I am heartily rejoiced that my
term is so near its close. I will soon
cease to be a servant and will
become a sovereign.

No President who performs his duties faithfully and conscientiously can have any leisure.

*O*ne great object of the Constitution in conferring upon the President a qualified negative upon the legislation of Congress was to protect minorities from injustice and oppression by majorities.

The President's power
is negative merely,
and not affirmative.

When it comes down to the
relations of any President with a
Congress controlled by the
opposite party, I just say this:
it is no bed of roses.

★ ★ ★

The passion for office among members of Congress is very great, if not absolutely disreputable, and greatly embarrasses the operations of the government. They create offices by their own votes and then seek to fill them themselves.

★★★★

Public opinion: May it always perform one of its appropriate offices; by teaching the public functionaries of the state and federal government that neither shall assume the exercise of powers entrusted by the Constitution to the other.

★★★★

★ ★ ★ ★ ★ ★ ★

Zachary Taylor

Born November 24, 1784 — Died July 9, 1850
12th President, 1849–1850 ★ Whig

*The axe, pick, saw and trowel,
has become more the implement
of the American soldier than the
cannon, musket or sword.*

*I*t would be judicious to act with magnanimity towards a prostrate foe.

I will not make myself
unhappy at what I cannot
prevent, nor give up the
Constitution or abandon
it because a rent has been
made in it, but will stick
by and repair it, and
nurse it as long as it will
hang together.

If I occupy the White House,
I must be untrammelled and
unpledged, so as to be
President of the nation and
not of a party.

★ ★ ★ ★ ★ ★ ★

Millard Fillmore

Born January 7, 1800 — Died March 8, 1874
13th President, 1850–1853 ★ Whig

*An honorable defeat is better than a
dishonorable victory.*

☆☆☆☆

God knows that I detest slavery, but it is an existing evil, for which we are not responsible, and we must endure it and give it such protection as is guaranteed by the Constitution, till we can get rid of it without destroying the last hope of free government in the world.

It is better to wear out
than rust out.

Wars will occur until man
changes his nature.

Church and state should be separate, not only in form, but fact—religion and politics should not be mingled.

$\mathcal{T}$he man who can look upon a crisis without being willing to offer himself upon the altar of his country is not fit for public trust.

★ ★ ★

$\mathcal{W}$ithout law there can be no real practical liberty, that when the law is trampled under foot tyranny rules, whether it appears in the form of a military despotism or of popular violence.

Millard Fillmore 87

The law is the only sure protection of the weak, and the only efficient restraint upon the strong.

Let us remember that revolutions do not always establish freedom. Our own free institutions were not the offspring of our revolution. They existed before.

★ ★ ★ ★ ★ ★ ★

Franklin Pierce

Born November 23, 1804 — Died October 8, 1869
14th President, 1853–1857 ★ Democrat

*I acknowledge my obligations
to the masses of my countrymen,
and to them alone.*

★★★★★

The revenue of the country,
levied almost insensibly to the
taxpayer, goes on from year to year,
increasing beyond either the
interests or the prospective wants
of the government.

I find that remark, "'Tis distance lends enchantment to the view" is no less true of the political than of the natural world.

If a man who has attained this high office cannot free himself from cliques and act independently, our Constitution is valueless.

*T*he storm of frenzy and faction
must inevitably dash itself
in vain against the unshaken
rock of the Constitution.

[on Congress]

In a body where there are more than one hundred talking lawyers ... you can make no calculation upon the termination of any debate and frequently, the more trifling the subject, the more animated and protracted the discussion.

We Polked you in '44,
We Shall Pierce you in '52.

A republic without parties is a complete anomaly. The history of all popular governments shows how absurd is the idea of their attempting to exist without parties.

★ ★ ★ ★ ★ ★ ★

James Buchanan

Born April 23, 1791 — Died June 1, 1868
15th President, 1857–1861 ★ Democrat

*The ballot box is the surest arbiter of
disputes among free men.*

Rest assured, that our population requires the curb more than the rein.

*L*et us look the danger fairly in the face.
Secession is neither more nor less
than revolution.

★ ★ ★

*S*elf-preservation is the first instinct of
nature, and therefore any state of society in
which the sword is all the time suspended
over the heads of the people must at last
become intolerable.

James Buchanan 97

☆☆☆☆

The march of free government on
this continent must not be
trammelled by the intrigues and
selfish interests of European powers.
Liberty must be allowed to work out its
natural results; and these will, ere long,
astonish the world.

☆☆☆☆

I acknowledge no master
but the law.

There is nothing stable
but heaven and the
Constitution.

What is right and what
is practicable are
two different things.

[*to Abraham Lincoln*]

If you are as happy, my dear sir,
on entering [the White House]
as I am in leaving it, you are the
happiest man in the country!

The distribution of patronage of the government is by far the most disagreeable duty of the President. Applicants are so numerous, and their applications are pressed with such eagerness by their friends both in and out of Congress, that the selection of one for any desirable office gives offense to many.

A long visit to a friend is often
a great bore. Never make
people twice glad.

What, sir! prevent the
American people from crossing the
Rocky Mountains? You might as
well command Niagara not to flow.
We must fulfill our destiny.

★ ★ ★ ★ ★ ★ ★

Abraham Lincoln

Born February 12, 1809 — Died April 15, 1865

16th President, 1861–1865 ★ Republican

If slavery is not wrong,
nothing is wrong.

☆☆☆☆☆

Character is like a tree and
reputation like its shadow.
The shadow is what we think of it;
the tree is the real thing.

☆☆☆☆☆

The best thing about the
future is that it comes only
one day at a time.

The Lord prefers
common-looking people.
That is the reason He makes
so many of them.

Abraham Lincoln

As I would not be a slave,
so I would not be a master. This
expresses my idea of democracy.

With malice toward none;
with charity for all;
with firmness in the right,
as God gives us to see
the right, let us strive on to
finish the work we
are in: to bind up the
nation's wounds.

I claim not to have controlled events, but confess plainly that events have controlled me.

Abraham Lincoln

*F*our score and seven years ago our fathers brought forth on this continent, a new nation, conceived in liberty, and dedicated to the proposition that all men are created equal. . . . [F]rom these honored dead we take increased devotion to that cause for which they gave the last full measure of devotion—that we here highly resolve that these dead shall not have died in vain—that this nation, under God, shall have a new birth of freedom—and that government of the people, by the people, for the people, shall not perish from the earth.

Abraham Lincoln   109

☆☆☆☆

[on the presidency]

You have heard the story . . . about
the man who was tarred and feathered
and carried out of town on a rail?
A man in the crowd asked him how he
liked it. His reply was if it was not
for the honor of the thing,
he would much rather walk.

[on meeting Harriet Beecher Stowe]

So you're the little woman
who wrote the book
that made this great war!

★ ★ ★

Such will be a great lesson of peace:
teaching men that what they
cannot take by an election,
neither can they take it by war.

Abraham Lincoln 111

The central idea of secession
is the essence of anarchy.

When you have got an
elephant by the hind leg,
and he is trying to run away,
it's best to let him run.

☆☆☆☆

I wish some of you would tell me the brand of whiskey that Grant drinks. I would like to send a barrel of it to my other generals.

☆☆☆☆

Abraham Lincoln   113

We shall nobly save,
or meanly lose, the last
best hope of earth.

When the hour comes for
dealing with slavery, I trust
I will be willing to do my duty
though it cost my life.

To sin by silence when
they should protest makes
cowards of men.

I have been told I was on the
road to hell, but I had no idea
it was just a mile down the road
with a dome on it.

☆☆☆☆☆

If you once forfeit the confidence of your fellow citizens, you can never regain their respect and esteem. It is true that you may fool all the people some of the time; you can even fool some of the people all the time; but you can't fool all of the people all the time.

★ ★ ★ ★ ★ ★ ★

Andrew Johnson

Born December 29, 1808—Died July 31, 1875
17th President, 1865–1869 ★ Democrat

*When I die, I desire no better
winding sheet than the Stars and Stripes,
and no softer pillow than the
Constitution of my country.*

☆☆☆☆

A railroad! It would frighten
horses, put the owners of public
vehicles out of business,
break up inns and taverns, and be
a monopoly generally.

☆☆☆☆

In the support and practice of correct principles we can never reach wrong results.

Away with slavery, the breeder of aristocrats. Up with the Stars and Stripes, symbol of free labor and free men.

Andrew Johnson 119

*H*onest conviction is my
courage, the Constitution
is my guide.

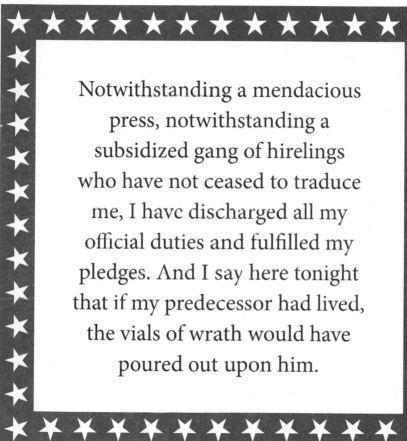

Notwithstanding a mendacious press, notwithstanding a subsidized gang of hirelings who have not ceased to traduce me, I have discharged all my official duties and fulfilled my pledges. And I say here tonight that if my predecessor had lived, the vials of wrath would have poured out upon him.

Secession is hell-born
and hell-bound.

If the rabble were lopped off
at one end and the aristocrat at
the other, all would be well
with the country.

★ ★ ★ ★ ★ ★ ★

Ulysses Simpson Grant

Born April 27, 1822 — Died July 23, 1885
18th President, 1869–1877 ★ Republican

*I know only two tunes; one of them is
"Yankee Doodle," and the other isn't.*

God gave us Lincoln and Liberty,
let us fight for both.

Ulysses Simpson Grant

The art of war is simple enough. Find out where your enemy is. Get at him as soon as you can. Strike him as hard as you can, and keep moving.

★ ★ ★

There never was a time when, in my opinion, some way could not be found to prevent the drawing of the sword.

Ulysses Simpson Grant 125

★ ★ ★

[on the surrender of General Robert E. Lee at Appomattox]

I felt like anything rather than rejoicing at the downfall of a foe who had fought so long and so valiantly.

I would suggest the taxation of all property equally whether church or corporation.

Wars produce many stories of fiction, some of which are told until they are believed to be true.

Whatever there is of greatness in the United States is due to labor. The laborer is the author of all greatness and wealth. Without labor there would be no government and no leading class.

★ ★ ★ ★ ★ ★ ★

Rutherford Birchard Hayes

Born October 4, 1822 — Died January 17, 1893
19th President, 1877–1881 ★ Republican

*Fighting battles is like courting girls:
those who make the most pretensions
and are boldest usually win.*

☆☆☆☆

I am not liked as a President
by the politicians in office, in the press,
or in Congress. But I am content
to abide the judgment—
the sober second thought—
of the people.

☆☆☆☆

130　*Rutherford Birchard Hayes*

"Practical politics" means
selfish ends promoted
by base means.

The melancholy thing
in our public life is the
insane desire to get higher.

He serves his party best who serves his country best.

★ ★ ★

The practice of annexing general legislation to appropriation has become a serious abuse. Every measure should stand on its own bottom.

★ ★ ★ ★ ★ ★ ★

James Abram Garfield

Born November 19, 1831 — Died September 19, 1881

20th President, 1881 (served six months) ★ Republican

*I would rather believe something and
suffer for it, than to slide along
into success without opinions.*

☆☆☆☆

An Englishman who was wrecked on a strange shore and wandering along the coast came to a gallows with a victim hanging on it, and fell down on his knees and thanked God that he at last beheld a sign of civilization.

A pound of pluck is worth
a ton of luck.

Things don't turn up
in this world until somebody
turns them up.

*I*deas are the great warriors
of the world, and a war
which has no ideas behind it,
is simply a brutality.

Real political issues cannot be manufactured by the leaders of political parties. The real political issues of the day declare themselves, and come out of the depths of that deep which we call public opinion.

I love agitation and investigation and glory in defending unpopular truth against popular error.

James Abram Garfield

*I*f you are not too large for
the place you now occupy,
you are too small for it.

★ ★ ★

*A*ssassination can be no more
guarded against than death by lightning;
and it is best not to worry about either.

James Abram Garfield

☆☆☆☆☆

It is alleged that in many communities Negro citizens are practically denied the freedom of the ballot. It is a crime which, if persisted in, will destroy the government itself.

☆☆☆☆☆

All free governments are party governments.

Justice and goodwill will outlast passion.

[on the presidency]

My God! What is there in this place that a man should ever want to get into it?

It had better be known in the outset whether the President is the head of the government, or the registering clerk of the Senate.

★ ★ ★ ★ ★ ★ ★

Chester Alan Arthur

Born October 5, 1829 — Died November 18, 1886
21st President, 1881–1885 ★ Republican

*Well, there doesn't seem to be
anything else for an ex-President to do
but go into the country and
raise big pumpkins.*

☆☆☆☆

No higher or more assuring proof
could exist of the strength and
permanence of popular government
than the fact that though the chosen
of the people be struck down,
his constitutional successor is
peacefully installed without shock
or strain except the sorrow which
mourns the bereavement.

☆☆☆☆

If it were not for the reporters,
I would tell you the truth.

I may be President of the
United States, but my private
life is nobody's damn business.

Chester Alan Arthur 145

★ ★ ★

If we heed the teachings of
history, we shall not forget that
in the life of every nation,
emergencies may arise when
a resort to arms can alone save
it from dishonor.

★ ★ ★ ★ ★ ★ ★

Grover Cleveland

Born March 18, 1837 — Died June 24, 1908
22nd & 24th President,
1885–1889 & 1893–1897 ★ Democrat

*A man is known by the company
he keeps, and also by the company from
which he is kept out.*

☆☆☆☆☆

I am not concerning myself about
what history will think, but contenting
myself with the approval of this fellow
named Cleveland whom I have
generally found to be a pretty
good sort of fellow.

☆☆☆☆☆

Party honesty is party
expediency.

No man has ever yet
been hanged for breaking
the spirit of a law.

$\mathcal{T}$he truly American sentiment
recognizes the dignity of
labor and the fact that honor
lies in honest toil.

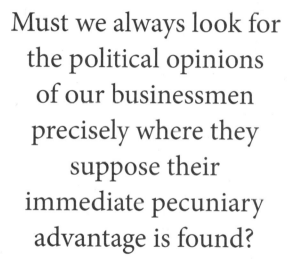

Must we always look for
the political opinions
of our businessmen
precisely where they
suppose their
immediate pecuniary
advantage is found?

Under our scheme of government the waste of public money is a crime against the citizen.

Grover Cleveland

I mistake the American people if they favor the odious doctrine that there is no such thing as international morality; that there is one law for a strong nation and another for a weak one.

Grover Cleveland 153

Whatever you do,
tell the truth.

He mocks the people who
propose that the
government shall protect the
rich and that they in turn
will care for the laboring poor.

★ ★ ★ ★ ★ ★ ★

Benjamin Harrison

Born August 20, 1833 — Died March 13, 1901
23rd President, 1889–1893 ★ Republican

*Public opinion is the most potent
monarch this world knows.*

☆☆☆☆

The manner by which women are treated is a good criterion to judge the true state of society. If we know but this one feature in a character of a nation, we may easily judge the rest, for as society advances, the true character of women is discovered.

Perhaps no emotion
cools sooner than that
of gratitude.

We Americans have no
commission from God to
police the world.

I want it understood that I am
the grandson of nobody.
I believe that every man should
stand on his own merits.

I believe also in the American opportunity which puts the starry sky above every boy's head, and sets his foot upon a ladder which he may climb until his strength gives out.

The law, the will of the majority expressed in orderly, constitutional methods, is the only king to which we bow.

*T*he indiscriminate denunciation of the rich is mischievous. It perverts the mind, poisons the heart and furnishes an excuse to crime. No poor man was ever made richer or happier by it. Not what a man has, but what he is, settles his class.

★ ★ ★

*H*ave you not learned that not stocks or bonds or stately homes, or products of mill or field are our country? It is the splendid thought that is in our minds.

Benjamin Harrison 161

Great lives do not go out.
They go on.

We must not forget
that it is often easier to
assemble armies than it is to
assemble army revenues.

With capability for war on
land and on sea unexcelled by
any nation in the world, we are
smitten by the love of peace.

Vacillation and inconsistency
are as incompatible with successful
diplomacy as they are with the
national dignity.

Benjamin Harrison   163

The Yankee intermingles with the Illinoisian, the Hoosier with the Sucker, and the people of the South with them all; and it is this commingling which gives that unity which marks the American nation.

★ ★ ★ ★ ★ ★

William McKinley

Born January 29, 1843 — Died September 14, 1901
25th President, 1897–1901 ★ Republican

Liberty to make our laws does not give us license to break them.

*O*ur differences are politics.
Our agreements are principles.

The ideals of yesterday
are the truths of today.

For labor a short day
is better than a short dollar.

★ ★ ★

[on the presidency, after two years in office]

I have had enough of it,
heaven knows. I have had
responsibilities enough
to kill any man.

★ ★ ★ ★ ★ ★ ★

Theodore Roosevelt

Born October 27, 1858 — Died January 6, 1919
26th President, 1901–1909 ★ Republican

The White House is a bully pulpit.

The things that will destroy America
are prosperity-at-any-price,
peace-at-any-price,
safety-first instead of duty-first,
the love of soft living and the
get-rich-quick theory of life.

Under government ownership
corruption can flourish
just as rankly as under
private ownership.

Don't hit at all if it's honorably
possible to avoid hitting;
but never hit soft!

[*on the presidency*]

It is fine to feel one's hand
guiding great machinery.

☆☆☆☆

A great democracy must be progressive or it will soon cease to be a great democracy.

☆☆☆☆

No people is wholly civilized
where a distinction is drawn
between stealing an office
and stealing a purse.

174   *Theodore Roosevelt*

To waste, destroy our natural resources, to skin and exhaust the land instead of using it so as to increase its usefulness, will result in undermining in the days of our children the very prosperity which we ought by right to hand down to them amplified and developed.

★ ★ ★

When you play, play hard; when you work, don't play at all.

Theodore Roosevelt 175

Wealth should be the servant
not the master of the people.

The reactionary is always
willing to take a
progressive attitude
on any issue that is dead.

☆☆☆☆☆

This country will not be a
good place for any of us
to live in unless we
make it a good place
for all of us to live in.

A man who has never gone to school
may steal from a freight car;
but if he has a university education,
he may steal the whole railroad.

The most successful politician
is he who says what everybody
is thinking most often
and in the loudest voice.

Nine-tenths of wisdom
consists in being
wise in time.

★ ★ ★

No President ever enjoyed
himself in the presidency
as much as I did.

Theodore Roosevelt 179

Actions speak louder than words.

Stand the gaff, play fair; be a good man to camp out with.

There is a homely adage which runs, "Speak softly and carry a big stick; you will go far." If the American nation will speak softly and yet build and keep at a pitch of the highest training a thoroughly efficient navy, the Monroe Doctrine will go far.

☆☆☆☆

A man who is good enough to shed
his blood for his country
is good enough to be given a
square deal afterwards. More than that
no man is entitled to, and less than
that no man shall have.

★ ★ ★ ★ ★ ★ ★

William Howard Taft

Born September 15, 1857 — Died March 8, 1930
27th President, 1909–1913 ★ Republican

*We often . . . find the law more honored
in the breach than in the observance.*

$\mathcal{I}$ am afraid I am a constant disappointment to my party. The fact of the matter is, the longer I am President the less of a party man I seem to become.

Machine politics and the spoils system are as much an enemy of a proper and efficient government system of civil service as the boll weevil is of the cotton crop.

☆☆☆☆

The President cannot make
clouds to rain and cannot make the
corn to grow, he cannot make
business good; although when these
things occur, political parties do claim
some credit for the good things that
have happened in this way.

Well, now I'm in the
White House, I'm not going to
be pushed around any more.

You cannot have a decent
government unless the majority
exercise the self-restraint
that men with great power
ought to exercise.

William Howard Taft 187

★ ★ ★

We live in a stage of politics, where legislators seem to regard the passage of laws as much more important than the results of their enforcement.

★ ★ ★ ★ ★ ★ ★

Woodrow Wilson

Born December 28, 1856 — Died February 3, 1924
28th President, 1913–1921 ★ Democrat

*The Constitution was not made to fit
us like a straitjacket. In its elasticity
lies its chief greatness.*

☆☆☆☆☆

The literary gift is a very dangerous gift to possess if you are not telling the truth, and I would a great deal rather, for my part, have a man stumble in his speech than to feel he was so exceedingly smooth that he had better be watched both day and night.

Woodrow Wilson

Uncompromising thought
is the luxury of the
closeted recluse.

If you want to make enemies,
try to change something.

Woodrow Wilson   191

When the representatives of
"Big Business" think of the people,
they do not include themselves.

The world must be made safe for democracy. Its peace must be planted upon the tested foundations of political liberty. We have no selfish ends to serve. We desire no conquest, no dominion. We seek no indemnities for ourselves, no material compensation for the sacrifices we shall freely make.

There is here a great melting pot in which we must compound a precious metal. That metal is the metal of nationality.

I have always been among those who believed that the greatest freedom of speech was the greatest safety, because if a man is a fool, the best thing to do is encourage him to advertise the fact by speaking.

★ ★ ★

I am not one of those who believe that a great standing army is the means of maintaining peace, because if you build up a great profession those who form parts of it want to exercise their profession.

Woodrow Wilson   195

☆☆☆☆

Self-determination is not a mere phrase. It is an imperative principle of action, which statesmen will henceforth ignore at their peril.

☆☆☆☆

One cool judgment is worth
a thousand hasty councils.
The thing to do is to supply
light and not heat.

If you think too much about
being reelected, it is very
difficult to be worth reelecting.

Woodrow Wilson 197

We are citizens of the world;
and the tragedy of our times
is that we do not know this.

People will endure their
tyrants for years, but they
tear their deliverers to pieces
if a millennium is not
created immediately.

★ ★ ★ ★ ★ ★ ★

Warren Gamaliel Harding

Born November 2, 1865 – Died August 2, 1923
29th President, 1921–1923 ★ Republican

Ambition is a commendable attribute,
without which no man succeeds.
Only inconsiderate ambition imperils.

☆☆☆☆☆

In the great fulfillment we must
have a citizenship less concerned about
what the government can do for it
and more anxious about
what it can do for the nation.

☆☆☆☆☆

200   *Warren Gamaliel Harding*

I don't know much about
Americanism, but it's a damn
good word with which
to carry an election.

Stabilize America first,
prosper America first,
think of America first and
exalt America first.

Warren Gamaliel Harding   201

I have said to the people
we mean to have less government
in business as well
as more business in government.

Frankly, being President is rather
an unattractive business unless one
relishes the exercise of power.
That is a thing which has never
greatly appealed to me.

202   *Warren Gamaliel Harding*

★ ★ ★ ★ ★ ★ ★

Calvin Coolidge

Born July 4, 1872 — Died January 5, 1933
30th President, 1923–1929 ★ Republican

Prosperity is only an instrument to be used,
not a deity to be worshipped.

☆☆☆☆

The power to tax is the power to destroy. A government which lays taxes on the people not required by urgent public necessity and sound public policy is not a protector of liberty, but an instrument of tyranny.

☆☆☆☆

I have noticed that nothing
I never said ever did me any harm.

I think the American public
wants a solemn ass as
President and I think I'll go
along with them.

*I*t is a great advantage to a President, and a major source of safety to the country, for him to know that he is not a great man.

I shall always consider it
the highest tribute
to my administration that
the opposition have based
so little of their criticism
on what I have really said
and done.

Never go out to meet trouble.
If you will just sit still, nine cases
out of ten, someone will intercept
it before it reaches you.

Calvin Coolidge

*T*here is no dignity quite so impressive,
and no independence quite so important,
as living within your means.

★ ★ ★

*N*othing is easier than spending public
money. It does not appear to belong
to anybody. The temptation is overwhelming
to bestow it on somebody.

Calvin Coolidge 209

War is the rule of force.
Peace is the reign of law.

[*on World War I*]
What the end of the four years
of carnage meant those
who remember it will never
forget and those who do not
can never be told.

★ ★ ★ ★ ★ ★ ★

Herbert Clark Hoover

Born August 10, 1874 — Died October 20, 1964
31st President, 1929–1933 ★ Republican

Being a politician is a poor profession.
Being a public servant is a noble one.

☆☆☆☆

Fishing is the chance to wash
one's soul with pure air. It brings
meekness and inspiration, reduces our
egotism, soothes our troubles,
and shames our wickedness. It is
discipline in the equality of men;
for all men are equal before fish.

☆☆☆☆

Herbert Clark Hoover

Two cars in every garage.

Blessed are the young,
for they shall inherit the
national debt.

Herbert Clark Hoover 213

*W*hen there is a lack of honor in government, the morals of the whole people are poisoned.

Once upon a time my
political opponents
honored me as possessing
the fabulous intellectual
and economic power
by which I created a
worldwide depression
all by myself.

No nation or individual
has been able to squander itself
into prosperity.

Herbert Clark Hoover

*E*ven if security from the cradle
to the grave could eliminate the risks of life,
it would be a dead hand on the creative spirit
of our people.

★ ★ ★

[*on the presidency*]

*T*he office in such times as these makes its
incumbent a repairman behind a dike.
No sooner is one leak plugged up than
it is necessary to dash over and stop another
that has broken out. There is no end to it.

Herbert Clark Hoover   217

No public man can be
just a little crooked.

Those who retire without
some occupation can spend
their time only in talking about
their ills and pills.

★ ★ ★ ★ ★ ★ ★

Franklin Delano Roosevelt

Born January 30, 1882 — Died April 12, 1945
32nd President, 1933–1945 ★ Democrat

When you get to the end of your rope,
tie a knot and hang on.

☆☆☆☆☆

Let me assert my firm belief that the only thing we have to fear is fear itself—nameless, unreasoning, unjustified terror which paralyzes needed efforts to convert retreat into advance.

☆☆☆☆☆

220   *Franklin Delano Roosevelt*

Never underestimate a man
who overestimates himself.

———★———

We have always known that
heedless self-interest was
bad morals; we know now that
it is bad economics.

Franklin Delano Roosevelt 221

I pledge you—I pledge myself—to a new deal for the American people.

We all know the story
of the unfortunate
chameleon which turned
brown when placed on
a brown rug, and turned
red when placed on a red
rug, but who died a tragic
death when they put him
on a Scotch plaid.

If we can "boondoggle" ourselves out of this depression, that word is going to be enshrined in the hearts of the American people for years to come.

Franklin Delano Roosevelt

*W*e must always be wary of those who with sounding brass and a tinkling cymbal preach the "ism" of appeasement. We must especially beware of that small group of selfish men who would clip the wings of the American eagle in order to feather their own nests.

★ ★ ★

*T*hose who would give up essential liberty to purchase a little temporary safety deserve neither liberty nor safety.

Franklin Delano Roosevelt   225

We must be the great
arsenal of democracy.

A just war in the long run
is far better for a man's soul than
the most prosperous peace.

People who are hungry and out of a job are the stuff of which dictatorships are made.

The ultimate failures of dictatorship cost humanity far more than any temporary failures of democracy.

Franklin Delano Roosevelt 227

Yesterday,
December 7, 1941—
a date which will live
in infamy—the
United States of America
was suddenly and
deliberately attacked
by naval and air forces
of the Empire of Japan.

We . . . would rather die
on our feet than live
on our knees.

[*on the presidency*]
The first twelve years
are the hardest.

★ ★ ★

There is a mysterious cycle
in human events. To some
generations much is given.
Of others much is expected.
This generation of
Americans has a rendezvous
with destiny.

Franklin Delano Roosevelt

★ ★ ★ ★ ★ ★ ★

Harry S Truman

Born May 8, 1884–Died December 26, 1972

33rd President, 1945–1953 ★ Democrat

*If you can't stand the heat,
get out of the kitchen.*

☆☆☆☆

I have appointed a Secretary of
Semantics—a most important post.
He is to furnish me with forty to fifty
dollar words. Tell me how to say yes
and no in the same sentence without
a contradiction. He is to tell me the
combination of words that will put me
against inflation in San Francisco
and for it in New York.

☆☆☆☆

If you want to live like a Republican, you've got to vote for a Democrat.

A President either is constantly on top of events, or if he hesitates, events will soon be on top of him.

Harry S Truman 233

$\mathcal{T}$he President is the representative of the whole nation and he's the only lobbyist that all one hundred and sixty million people in this country have.

These men who live in the past remind me of a toy . . . a small wooden bird called the Floogie Bird. Around the Floogie Bird's neck is a label reading: "I fly backwards. I don't care where I'm going. I just want to see where I've been."

☆☆☆☆

A politician is a man who understands government, and it takes a politician to run a government. A statesman is a politician who's been dead ten or fifteen years.

☆☆☆☆

About the meanest thing you
can say about a man is that
he means well.

It was said in the First World War
that the French fought for their
country, the British fought for
freedom of the seas, and the
Americans fought for souvenirs.

Harry S Truman 237

Being a President is like riding a tiger. A man has to keep on riding or be swallowed.

238   *Harry S Truman*

The President hears a hundred voices telling him that he is the greatest man in the world. He must listen carefully indeed to hear the one voice that tells him he is not.

★ ★ ★

Three things ruin a man. Power, money, and women. I never wanted power. I never had any money, and the only woman in my life is up at the house right now.

Harry S Truman   239

If you can't convince them,
confuse them.

It's a recession when your
neighbor loses his job,
it's a depression when
you lose your own.

I always quote an epitaph on a
tombstone in a cemetery in
Tombstone, Arizona:
"Here lies Jack Williams. He done
his damnedest." I think that is the
greatest epitaph a man can have. . .
and that is what I have tried to do.

Harry S Truman   241

The buck stops here.

I am getting ready to see
Stalin and Churchill and it is a
chore. I have to take my tuxedo,
tails, preacher coat, high hat,
low hat and hard hat.

★ ★ ★ ★ ★ ★ ★

Dwight David Eisenhower

Born October 14, 1890 — Died March 28, 1969

34th President, 1953–1961 ★ Republican

Neither a wise man nor a brave man lies down on the tracks of history to wait for the train of the future to run over him.

★★★★

In the councils of government,
we must guard against the acquisition
of unwarranted influence,
whether sought or unsought,
by the military-industrial complex.
The potential for the disastrous rise of
misplaced power exists and will persist.

244   *Dwight David Eisenhower*

The opportunist thinks of me and today. The statesman thinks of us and tomorrow.

There are a number of things wrong with Washington. One of them is that everyone has been too long away from home.

Dwight David Eisenhower 245

What counts is not the size of the dog in the fight but the size of the fight in the dog.

Every gun that is made,
every warship launched,
every rocket fired
signifies, in the final sense,
a theft from those who
hunger and are not fed,
those who are cold and
are not clothed.

The only way to win
World War III is to prevent it.

Dwight David Eisenhower

*M*en acquainted with the battlefield
will not be found among the numbers
that glibly talk of another war.

★ ★ ★

I think that people want peace so much
that one of these days governments
had better get out of the way and
let them have it.

Dwight David Eisenhower 249

[on the atomic bomb]
It is not enough to take this weapon
out of the hands of soldiers.
It must be put into the hands
of those who will know how to
strip its military casing and
adapt it to the arts of peace.

Under the cloud of
threatening war, it is humanity
hanging from a cross of iron.

Whatever America hopes
to bring to pass in this world
must first come to pass in
the heart of America.

Dwight David Eisenhower   251

The search for a scapegoat is the easiest of all hunting expeditions.

A people that values its privileges above its principles soon loses both.

Dwight David Eisenhower

★ ★ ★ ★ ★ ★ ★

John Fitzgerald Kennedy

Born May 29, 1917 — Died November 22, 1963

35th President, 1961–1963 ★ Democrat

*And so, my fellow Americans: ask not
what your country can do for you —
ask what you can do for your country.*

☆☆☆☆

[remark made at a 1962 White House dinner honoring Nobel Laureates]

I think this is the most extraordinary collection of talent, of human knowledge, that has ever been gathered together at the White House—
with the possible exception of when Thomas Jefferson dined alone.

John Fitzgerald Kennedy

Politics is like football.
If you see daylight,
go through the hole.

[*describing himself*]
An idealist without illusions.

Victory has a hundred fathers,
but defeat is an orphan.

Those of you who regard
my profession of political life
with some disdain should
remember that it made it
possible for me to move from
being an obscure lieutenant
in the United States Navy to
Commander in Chief in
fourteen years with very little
technical competence.

[on becoming a World War II hero]

It was involuntary.
They sank my boat.

★ ★ ★

I have just received the following telegram from my generous daddy. It says, "Dear Jack: Don't buy a single vote more than is necessary. I'll be damned if I'm going to pay for a landslide."

Too often we . . . enjoy the comfort of opinion without the discomfort of thought.

War will exist until that distant day when the conscientious objector enjoys the same reputation and prestige that the warrior does today.

John Fitzgerald Kennedy 259

When we got into office, the thing that surprised me most was to find that things were just as bad as we'd been saying they were.

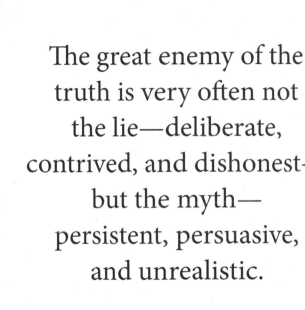

The great enemy of the truth is very often not the lie—deliberate, contrived, and dishonest—but the myth—persistent, persuasive, and unrealistic.

We cannot expect that all nations will adopt like systems, for conformity is the jailer of freedom and the enemy of growth.

John Fitzgerald Kennedy

$\mathscr{H}$istory is a relentless master.
It has no present, only the past rushing
into the future. To try to hold fast
is to be swept aside.

★ ★ ★

$\mathscr{T}$he courage of life is often a less
dramatic spectacle than the courage of a final
moment; but it is no less than a
magnificent mixture of triumph and tragedy.

John Fitzgerald Kennedy   263

Liberty without learning
is always in peril and
learning without liberty
is always in vain.

★ ★ ★

In the past, those who
foolishly sought power by
riding the back of the tiger
ended up inside.

★ ★ ★ ★ ★ ★ ★

Lyndon Baines Johnson

Born August 27, 1908 — Died January 22, 1973

36th President, 1963–1969 ★ Democrat

Politics is the art of the possible.

☆☆☆☆

The Secretary of Labor is in
charge of finding you a job,
the Secretary of the Treasury is in
charge of taking half the money
away from you, and the
Attorney General is in charge of
suing you for the other half.

There is but one way for a President to deal with the Congress, and that is continuously, incessantly, and without interruption.

———————★———————

Words wound. But as a veteran of twelve years in the U.S. Senate, I happily attest they do not kill.

Lyndon Baines Johnson 267

*W*e did not choose to be the
guardians at the gate.
But there is no one else.

In 1790, the nation which had fought a revolution against taxation without representation discovered that some of its citizens weren't much happier about taxation with representation.

Giving a man a chance to work and feed his family and provide for his children does not destroy his initiative. Hunger destroys initiative. Ignorance destroys initiative. A cold and indifferent government destroys initiative.

270   *Lyndon Baines Johnson*

*I*f you're in politics and you can't tell when you walk into a room who's for you and who's against you, then you're in the wrong line of work.

★ ★ ★

*I*t is easier today to buy a destructive weapon, a gun, in a hardware store, than it is to vote.

Lyndon Baines Johnson 271

War is always the same. It is young men dying in the fullness of their promise. It is trying to kill a man that you do not even know well enough to hate. Therefore, to know war is to know that there is still madness in this world.

Poverty has many roots,
but the tap root is ignorance.

We must be constantly prepared
for the worst and constantly
acting for the best — strong enough
to win a war and wise enough
to prevent one.

Lyndon Baines Johnson   273

The world is engaged in
a race between education
and chaos.

Once we considered
education a public
expense; we know now that
it is a public investment.

★ ★ ★ ★ ★ ★ ★

Richard Milhous Nixon

Born January 9, 1913 — Died April 22, 1994
37th President, 1969–1974 ★ Republican

A man is not finished when he's defeated;
he's finished when he quits.

☆☆☆☆

[on accepting the Republican presidential nomination, 1968]

Let us begin by committing ourselves
to the truth—to see it like it is,
and tell it like it is—to find the truth,
to speak the truth, and to live the truth.

☆☆☆☆

Neutrality where the
Communists are concerned
means three things: we get out;
they stay in; they take over.

Communist leaders believe
in Lenin's precept:
Probe with bayonets.
If you encounter mush, proceed;
if you encounter steel, withdraw.

Richard Milhous Nixon 277

If any individual wants to be a leader and isn't controversial, that means he never stood for anything.

[on the first moon landing, July 20, 1969]

For years politicians have promised
the moon—I'm the first one
to be able to deliver it.

★ ★ ★

I believe in building bridges
but we should build only our
end of the bridge.

Richard Milhous Nixon 279

I learned a great deal from a football coach who not only taught his players how to win but also taught them that when you lose you don't quit, that when you lose you fight harder the next time.

I'm an introvert in an
extrovert's profession.

In dealing with the environment
we must learn not how to master
nature but how to master
ourselves, our institutions,
and our technology.

Richard Milhous Nixon   281

President Eisenhower's whole life is proof of the stark but simple truth— that no one hates war more than one who has seen a lot of it.

282   *Richard Milhous Nixon*

The Chinese use two brush strokes
to write the word "crisis." One brush stroke
stands for danger; the other for opportunity.
In a crisis, be aware of the danger—
but recognize the opportunity.

★ ★ ★

Those who hate you don't win
unless you hate them. And then you
destroy yourself.

Richard Milhous Nixon 283

When the President does it, that means it is not illegal.

Once you get into this great stream of history, you can't get out.

★ ★ ★ ★ ★ ★ ★

Gerald Rudolph Ford

Born July 14, 1913 — Died December 26, 2006
38th President, 1974–1977 ★ Republican

*Truth is the glue that holds governments
together. Compromise is the oil
that makes governments go.*

Only eight months ago,
when I last stood here, I told you
I was a Ford, not a Lincoln.
Tonight I say I am still a Ford,
but I am not a Model T.

[*on his pardon of Richard Nixon*]
It can go on and on, or someone
must write "The End" to it.
I have concluded that only I can
do that. And if I can, I must.

[*on his presidency*]

I guess it just proves that in America anyone can be President.

To me the presidency and
vice-presidency were not prizes
to be won but a duty to be done.

The three-martini lunch is the
epitome of American efficiency.
Where else can you get an earful,
a bellyful and a snootful
at the same time?

288   *Gerald Rudolph Ford*

★ ★ ★ ★ ★ ★ ★

James Earl Carter

Born October 1, 1924
39th President, 1977–1981 ★ Democrat

*America did not invent human rights.
In a very real sense . . . human rights
invented America.*

*W*e should live our lives as though
Christ were coming this afternoon.

We've uncovered some embarrassing ancestors in the not too distant past. Some horse thieves, and some people killed on Saturday nights. One of my relatives, unfortunately, was even in the newspaper business.

★★★★☆

The tax system is a disgrace to the human race. . . . It's a scandal that a businessman can deduct his fifty-dollar lunch but a worker can't deduct the sandwich in his lunch pail.

★★★★☆

A simple and proper function
of government is just to make it easy
for us to do good and difficult
for us to do wrong.

We must adjust to
changing times and still hold to
unchanging principles.

James Earl Carter   293

The best way to enhance freedom in other lands is to demonstrate here that our democratic system is worthy of emulation.

294   *James Earl Carter*

*W*e were sure that ours was a nation
of the ballot, not the bullet, until the murders
of John Kennedy, Robert Kennedy,
and Martin Luther King, Jr.

★ ★ ★

*I*f you fear making anyone mad, then
you ultimately probe for the lowest common
denominator of human achievement.

James Earl Carter 295

Whatever starts in California unfortunately has an inclination to spread.

I can get up at nine and be rested, or I can get up at six and be President.

★ ★ ★ ★ ★ ★ ★

Ronald Wilson Reagan

Born February 6, 1911 — Died June 5, 2004
40th President, 1981–1989 ★ Republican

*Governments have a tendency not to solve
problems, only to rearrange them.*

☆☆☆☆

If I could paraphrase a well-known statement by Will Rogers that he never met a man he didn't like—I'm afraid we have some people around here who never met a tax they didn't hike.

☆☆☆☆

I'm proud to be called a pig.
It stands for pride, integrity,
and guts.

Government exists to protect
us from each other. We can't afford
the government it would take to
protect us from ourselves.

Ronald Wilson Reagan   299

*W*hat I'd really like to do
is go down in history as the
President who made Americans
believe in themselves again.

Freedom is never more than one generation away from extinction. We didn't pass it to our children in the bloodstream. It must be fought for, protected, and handed on for them to do the same, or one day we will spend our sunset years telling our children and our children's children what it was once like in the United States where men were free.

☆☆☆☆

The Chinese philosopher, Sun Tzu, 2,500 years ago said winning a hundred victories in a hundred battles is not the acme of skill; to subdue the enemy without fighting is the acme of skill.

☆☆☆☆

I have always stated that the nearest thing to eternal life we'll ever see on this earth is a government program.

Inflation is as violent as a mugger, as frightening as an armed robber and as deadly as a hit man.

Ronald Wilson Reagan   303

Nations do not mistrust
each other because they are
armed; they are armed because
they mistrust each other.

Ronald Wilson Reagan

$\mathcal{I}$ will not make age an issue
in this campaign. I am not going to exploit,
for political purposes, my opponent's
youth and inexperience.

★ ★ ★

$\mathcal{I}$ used to say that politics was
the second-oldest profession.
I have come to know that it bears a
gross similarity to the first.

Ronald Wilson Reagan　305

The taxpayer—that's someone who works for the federal government but doesn't have to take a civil service exam.

★ ★ ★

Regimes planted by bayonets do not take root.

★ ★ ★ ★ ★ ★ ★

George Herbert Walker Bush

Born June 12, 1924

41st President, 1989–1993 ★ Republican

*If anyone tells you that America's
best days are behind her,
they're looking the wrong way.*

☆☆☆☆☆

America is never wholly herself
unless she is engaged in high moral
principle. We as a people have such
a purpose today. It is to make
kinder the face of the nation and
gentler the face of the world.

This is a fact: Strength in the pursuit of peace is no vice; isolation in the pursuit of security is no virtue.

Leadership to me means duty, honor, country. It means character, and it means listening from time to time.

George Herbert Walker Bush   309

*C*ommunism died this year. . . .
The biggest thing that has happened
in the world in my life, in our lives,
is this: By the grace of God,
America won the cold war.

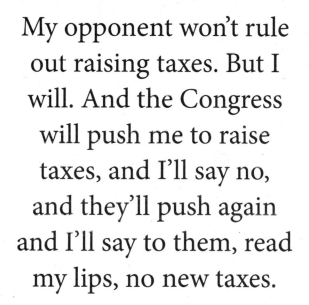

My opponent won't rule out raising taxes. But I will. And the Congress will push me to raise taxes, and I'll say no, and they'll push again and I'll say to them, read my lips, no new taxes.

This is America . . . a brilliant
diversity spread like stars.
Like a thousand points of light
in a broad and peaceful sky.

George Herbert Walker Bush

T have spoken of a thousand points of light—of all the community organizations that are spread like stars throughout the nation, doing good. The old ideas are new again because they are not old, they are timeless: duty, sacrifice, commitment, and a patriotism that finds its expression in taking part and pitching in.

★ ★ ★

A government that remembers that the people are its master is a good and needed thing.

George Herbert Walker Bush   313

★ ★ ★

The notion of political correctness
has ignited controversy across the land.
And although the movement arises
from the laudable desire to sweep
away the debris of racism and sexism
and hatred, it replaces old prejudices
with new ones. . . . What began as a
crusade for civility has soured into a
cause of conflict and even censorship.

314   *George Herbert Walker Bush*

★ ★ ★ ★ ★ ★ ★

William Jefferson Clinton

Born August 19, 1946

42nd President, 1993–2001 ★ Democrat

*There is nothing wrong in America
that can't be fixed with what
is right in America.*

☆☆☆☆☆

Education is about more than making
money and mastering technology,
even in the twenty-first century. It's about
making connections and mastering
the complexities of the world. It's about
seeing the world as it is and advancing the
cause of human dignity.

William Jefferson Clinton

I want a leaner, not a meaner, government.

The future is not an inheritance, it is an opportunity and an obligation.

William Jefferson Clinton   317

$\mathcal{I}$ refuse to be part of a generation that celebrates the death of communism abroad with the loss of the American dream at home.

For too long we've been told about "us" and "them." Each and every election we see a new slate of arguments and ads telling us that "they" are the problem, not "us." But there can be no "them" in America. There's only us.

The best social program
is a good job.

I did not run for this job just
to warm the seat. I desperately
want to make a difference.

The world wars are over.
The cold war has been won.
Now it is our job to win the peace.

The real American heroes today
are the citizens who get up every
morning and have the courage to
work hard and play by the rules.

322 *William Jefferson Clinton*

*I*f you live long enough, you'll make mistakes. But if you learn from them, you'll be a better person. It's how you handle adversity, not how it affects you. The main thing is never quit, never quit, never quit.

★ ★ ★

*W*e must do what America does best: offer more opportunity to all and demand more responsibility from all.

William Jefferson Clinton   323

[remarking on the reception to his lengthy speech at the 1988 Democratic Convention]

It wasn't my finest hour.
It wasn't even my finest
hour and a half.

I don't suppose there's any
public figure that's ever been
subject to any more violent
personal attacks than I have.

★ ★ ★ ★ ★ ★ ★

George Walker Bush

Born July 6, 1946

43rd President, 2001–2009 ★ Republican

*Whether we bring our enemies to justice,
or bring justice to our enemies,
justice will be done.*

Terrorist attacks can shake the foundations of our biggest buildings, but they cannot touch the foundation of America. These acts shatter steel, but they cannot dent the steel of American resolve.

Some folks look at me and see
a certain swagger, which in
Texas is called "walking."

The true history of my
administration will be written fifty
years from now, and you and
I will not be around to see it.

★ ★ ★

When an eighteen-year-old
Palestinian girl is induced
to blow herself up and in
the process kills a
seventeen year-old Israeli girl,
the future itself is dying . . .

★ ★ ★ ★ ★ ★ ★

Barack Hussein Obama

Born August 4, 1961

44th President, 2009– ★ Democrat

There's not a liberal America and a conservative America; there's the United States of America.

☆☆☆☆☆

To those leaders around the globe who seek
to sow conflict, or blame their society's
ills on the West—know that your people
will judge you on what you can build, not
what you destroy. To those who cling to
power through corruption and deceit and
the silencing of dissent, know that you are
on the wrong side of history; but that we
will extend a hand if you are willing to
unclench your fist.

☆☆☆☆☆

330   *Barack Hussein Obama*

My job is not to represent
Washington to you, but to
represent you to Washington.

I'm asking you to believe.
Not just in my ability to bring about
real change in Washington . . .
I'm asking you to believe in yours.

$\mathcal{T}$oday I say to you that the challenges we face are real, they are serious and they are many. They will not be met easily or in a short span of time. But know this America: They will be met.

And so, to all other peoples and governments . . . from the grandest capitals to the small village where my father was born: know that America is a friend of each nation and every man, woman and child who seeks a future of peace and dignity, and we are ready to lead once more.

I don't oppose all wars.
What I am opposed to is a dumb
war. . . . A rash war. A war based not
on reason but on passion, not on
principle but on politics.

Barack Hussein Obama

*W*hen I am President, I will make it absolutely clear that working in an Obama Administration is not about serving your former employer, your future employer, or your bank account—it's about serving your country, and that's what comes first.

★ ★ ★

*O*n my very first day as President, I will launch the most sweeping ethics reform in history to make the White House the people's house and send the Washington lobbyists back to K Street.

Barack Hussein Obama 335

*T*hey can say that this was the
time when America learned
to dream again.

I think we've all had enough. Enough of
the broken promises. Enough of the
failed leadership. Enough of the can't-do,
won't-do, won't-even-try style of governance.

We will return government
to the people by bringing government
to the people—by making it open and
transparent so that anyone can see that our
business is the people's business.

Barack Hussein Obama   337

★ ★ ★

[*on America*]

It's the hope of slaves sitting around a fire singing freedom songs; the hope of immigrants setting out for distant shores . . . the hope of a skinny kid with a funny name who believes that America has a place for him, too. The audacity of hope!

Index